GETTING TO KNOW THE WORLD'S GREATEST
INVENTORS & SCIENTISTS

# LISE
# MEITNER

Had the Right Vision about Nuclear Fission

WRITTEN AND ILLUSTRATED BY MIKE VENEZIA

CHILDREN'S PRESS®
AN IMPRINT OF SCHOLASTIC INC.
NEW YORK   TORONTO   LONDON   AUCKLAND   SYDNEY
MEXICO CITY   NEW DELHI   HONG KONG
DANBURY, CONNECTICUT

Reading Consultant: Nanci R. Vargus, EdD, Assistant Professor, School of Education, University of Indianapolis

Science Consultant: Doug Welch, PhD, McMaster University, Hamilton, Ontario

Photographs © 2010: American Institute of Physics, Emilio Segrè Visual Archives, Physics Today Collection: 31 (Robert Davis); Courtesy of Archiv der Max-Planck-Gesellschaft, Berlin-Dahlem: 17, 19; Art Resource, NY/DeA Picture Library: 25; Bridgeman Art Library International Ltd., London/New York: 14 (Bibliotheque des Arts Decoratifs, Paris, France/Archives Charmet), 24 (Private Collection/Archives Charmet); Courtesy of Churchill Archives Centre, Churchill College, Cambridge: 8 (Lise Meitner Papers/MTNR 8/4/1); Corbis Images: 3, 16 (Bettmann), 27 (Tibor Bognar), 22 (Bek Shakirov/Images.com), 30; DK Images: 23; The Granger Collection, New York: 15 (ullstein bild), 10, 20; The Image Works/Photo 12: 21.

Colorist for illustrations: Andrew Day

Library of Congress Cataloging-in-Publication Data

Venezia, Mike.
  Lise Meitner : had the right vision about nuclear fission / written and illustrated by Mike Venezia.
      p. cm. — (Getting to know the world's greatest inventors and scientists)
  Includes index.
  ISBN-13: 978-0-531-23702-1 (lib. bdg.)  978-0-531-20776-5 (pbk.)
  ISBN-10:  0-531-23702-8 (lib. bdg.)      0-531-20776-5 (pbk.)
  1. Meitner, Lise, 1878-1968—Juvenile literature. 2. Physicists—Germany—Biography—Juvenile literature. 3. Women Physicists—Germany—Biography—Juvenile literature. 4. Nuclear Fission—Juvenile literature. I. Title. II. Series.

  QC774.M4V46 2010
  539.7092—dc22
  [B]

2009000358

1 2 3 4 5 6 7 8 9 10 R 19 18 17 16 15 14 13 12 11 10          62

Nuclear physicist Lise Meitner in the 1930s

Lise Meitner was born in Vienna, Austria, in 1878. Lise was a pioneer in the new science of **nuclear physics.** At the beginning of the twentieth century, scientists were just starting to unlock the secrets of the **atom.** Atoms are incredibly tiny building blocks that make up everything on Earth. In 1939, Lise Meitner made an important discovery about the atom that would change the history of the world.

It has never been easy for scientists to learn
about atoms and how they work. Atoms
are so small that they can be seen only with
special, powerful microscopes. In the early
1900s, when Lise Meitner began studying
nuclear physics in college, such microscopes
hadn't been invented yet. Many scientists
still refused to believe that atoms actually
existed. They thought that things that couldn't

be seen simply didn't exist. These scientists
looked down on professors and students who
studied atoms and **radioactivity**—an invisible
form of energy released by certain atoms.
They thought it was a big waste of time. That
didn't bother Lise and her colleagues, though.
They were convinced atoms existed and were
determined to find out more about them.

There were other hurdles that got in the way of Lise's search for scientific discoveries. One of the biggest was that Lise was a girl. In Vienna during the 1800s, girls went to school only until they finished grade school. They were then expected to learn how to find a husband, run a household, and raise a family. If a girl wanted to become a lawyer, doctor, or scientist, like Lise did, it was almost impossible. Fortunately, Lise's parents understood the importance of education. They encouraged all eight of their children to learn as much as possible.

By the time Lise was eight years old, she was totally into reading and learning. Her favorite subjects were math and science. Lise often fell asleep with a math book or science book by her side or under her pillow.

Nine-year-old Lise Meitner (holding doll) with her family in 1887

Girls weren't allowed to attend public high school in Vienna, but Lise's father agreed to send Lise to a private school. By the time she graduated from the all-girls school, Lise was happy to find that the rules that kept women from attending universities were beginning to change. Now, if a woman could pass a difficult entrance exam, she would be allowed to attend a college. Lise didn't want to risk this opportunity. For two years, she studied harder than ever—day and night.

Lise passed the exam. In 1901, she became the second woman to enter the University of Vienna's physics department. Lise was overjoyed, but it would take a while before people at the university would get used to having a woman around.

Lise couldn't wait to learn everything she could about physics. Physics is the science that deals with **matter** and energy and how they interact. It includes the study of light, heat, sound, and motion. Lise was fortunate to have her first classes with an amazing professor, Dr. Ludwig Boltzmann. Not only was Professor Boltzmann certain that atoms existed, he also believed that women could achieve as much as men in the field of science.

Ludwig Boltzmann was one of Lise's most influential teachers.

Because physics was a fairly new science at the time, the university didn't put a lot of money into it. Lise's physics classes were held in an old, broken-down apartment building that Lise thought was a firetrap. But it was in this building that Professor Boltzmann inspired his students to become great scientists.

In 1906, Lise graduated from the University of Vienna with a doctoral degree and highest honors. Even so, because of **prejudice** against women, Lise couldn't find a job. There weren't any positions open for women scientists anywhere in Austria. Lise was allowed to continue her experiments in the university's lab, but she was never paid for her work.

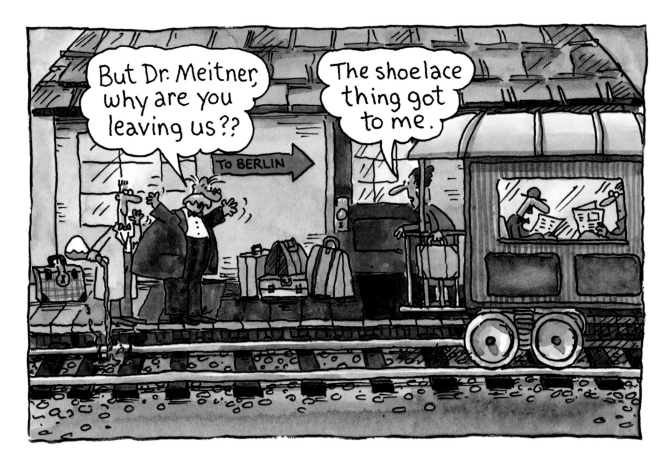

Lise realized that if she wanted to have a career in science, she would have to leave Vienna. She knew that the best place for her to continue her studies would be at the University of Berlin in Germany. If Lise could get admitted to that university, she could learn a lot more about physics.

Lise was inspired by the work of Marie and Pierre Curie.

Lise always kept up on the latest physics news of the day. She was particularly interested in the exciting discoveries Marie and Pierre Curie were making. Marie was Lise's hero. She was a chemist and physicist who worked in France. She and her husband Pierre discovered a radioactive **element** called radium. An element is a pure substance that can't be separated into anything else. Iron, gold, oxygen, and radium are a few examples of the more than one hundred elements that have been discovered so far.

Radium gave off mysterious, powerful rays. Marie and Pierre were busy trying to find out what caused the rays. This was the kind of scientific study Lise dreamed of doing.

The University of Berlin had some of the most famous physics professors in the world. Lise hoped to continue her experiments in the university's modern and well-equipped laboratories. When Lise arrived in Berlin, she went to see the head of the physics department, Dr. Max Planck. Like most professors, Max wasn't crazy about including women in his classes, but Lise was determined to change his mind.

This is how Berlin looked when Lise arrived there in 1907.

Lise impressed Professor Planck with her knowledge of physics. She also showed him some important experiments she had worked on. Max Planck decided to give Lise a chance. Lise was thrilled. She deepened her understanding of physics in Max Planck's advanced classes.

Lise also got to meet another brilliant scientist in Berlin: Otto Hahn. Otto was a chemist who was known for his experiments with radioactive materials. Otto was looking for a partner, and

Lise seemed to be just the right person. Lise had planned to spend only a few months in Germany. But the opportunity to work with Otto Hahn on radioactive experiments was too exciting to turn down. Lise ended up staying in Berlin and working with Otto for thirty years!

Otto Hahn (front row, second from left) and Lise Meitner with fellow scientists at the University of Berlin in 1909

Otto and Lise were perfect research partners. Lise had always been a quiet, shy, and very serious person. Otto was just the opposite. He loved going to parties and telling jokes. Sometimes, Otto would play practical jokes on Lise. He wanted to get her to lighten up and enjoy life more.

Otto Hahn and Lise Meitner in the lab at the University of Berlin

Otto Hahn and Lise Meitner were very successful with their lab experiments. Together, they discovered a new element they called protactinium. Protactinium is a radioactive element. Like radium, it gave off mysterious, invisible rays of energy. Scientists suspected that the radioactive energy was due to the breaking apart of some of the atoms.

Unfortunately, Lise's study of radioactivity and the secrets of the atom were interrupted when World War I began. Germans hoped the war would strengthen Germany's power in Europe. Lise did her part by becoming a nurse. She traveled to dangerous battle zones to help save soldiers' lives.

This photograph shows German troops leaving Berlin to go off to war in 1914.

During World War I, Lise worked as a nurse, helping wounded German soldiers like these.

Lise was horrified by the sight of so many suffering and dying soldiers. In 1918, Germany was defeated, and the war ended. Lise was relieved to return to her work. Over the next few years, as Germany struggled to recover from the war's destruction, Lise Meitner finally started to become recognized for her important work. The University of Berlin made her a professor—Germany's first woman professor.

In the early 1900s, new discoveries about the atom were being made all the time. Scientists found that the atom wasn't a solid particle, as they had once believed. They now knew the atom had a center, called a **nucleus,** which was circled by **electrons.** Electrons have a negative electrical charge. Then scientists discovered that an atom's nucleus contains a mix of two kinds of **particles.** These are **protons,** which have a positive electrical charge, and **neutrons,** which are neutral—they have no charge at all. These particles work together to hold the atom's nucleus together.

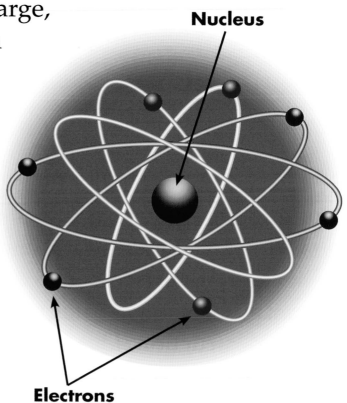

**Nucleus**

**Electrons**

This diagram shows electrons orbiting the nucleus of an atom.

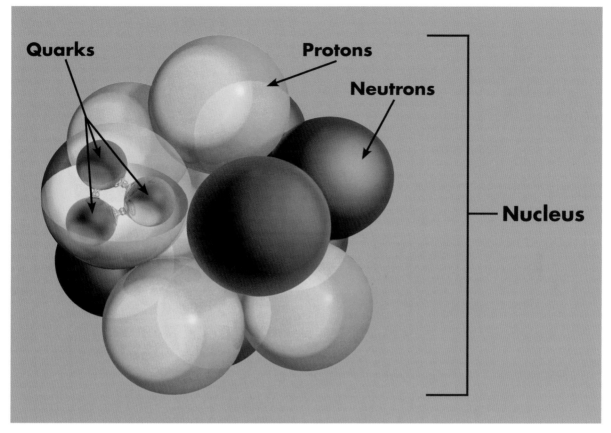

As this diagram shows, the nucleus of an atom is made up of protons (yellow) and neutrons (purple). In the 1960s, scientists discovered that protons and neutrons were made up of even smaller particles, called quarks (red, blue, and green).

Knowing more about the workings of atoms helped scientists do some exciting new experiments that were based on the work of world-renowned physicist Albert Einstein. In 1905, Einstein had theorized that huge amounts of energy could be released from an atom if there was some way to break apart its nucleus.

When dictator Adolf Hitler (right) came to power, Germany became a dangerous place for Jews and many other people. In 1938, Lise Meitner escaped to Holland and then to Sweden.

Lise was anxious to start investigating the latest atomic discoveries. But in the 1930s, the situation in Germany changed dramatically. In 1933, a **dictator** named Adolf Hitler took power. Hitler and his Nazi Party wanted to take over Europe—and possibly the world. Moreover, Hitler hated Jewish people—and Lise came from a Jewish family.

Hitler gradually took more and more rights away from Jews in Germany. Lise noticed that Jewish chemists and physicists were all losing their jobs. She was horrified to learn that many German Jews were being sent away to concentration camps—and even murdered.

Lise got out of Germany just in time. After World War II started in 1939, Hitler sent millions of Jews, like these, to concentration camps, where most of them were killed.

By 1938, Lise knew she had to get out of Germany. But Adolf Hitler wasn't letting Jewish people leave. Luckily, Lise's friends arranged to sneak her out of the country. It was a risky move, but Lise made it to safety.

Lise managed to escape to Holland, and eventually to Sweden. She missed her home and her friends in Germany very much. Lise was happy, though, to have frequent visits from her nephew, Otto Frisch. Lise was very proud of her nephew. He had become a respected scientist, too. Lise also kept in touch with Otto Hahn. As the war heated up, Lise and Otto wrote to each other about their latest experiments. Soon, Lise would make her most important discovery.

Stockholm, Sweden (above), became Lise's home during the war. She and Otto Hahn continued their research by writing letters to each other.

In one letter, Otto wrote to Lise about a puzzling mystery. During one of his experiments with a radioactive element called uranium, the uranium seemed to change into a different element. This seemed impossible! Lise thought long and hard about Otto's letter. One evening, while strolling in the snowy countryside and talking with her nephew, Lise came up with a big idea. She believed that Otto, without knowing it, had found a way to chip away at a uranium atom's nucleus. Lise thought that the uranium atom split apart, forming new elements and releasing energy.

Lise sat down on a log and made some calculations that showed exactly how her theory worked. Together, Lise and her nephew wrote an important letter in which

they used the term "fission" to describe the process of splitting an atom's nucleus. Later, Lise's description of how atoms can be made to split apart and release huge amounts of energy was shown to be correct.

Lise realized immediately that **nuclear fission** could be used in a horrible way. If scientists could release great amounts of energy from atoms, they could create enormous explosions. Indeed, scientists soon began working on creating the first **atomic bomb.** Lise was invited to take part

This photograph shows the testing of an atomic bomb in 1954. Lise was greatly saddened that her discoveries led to the creation of such a destructive weapon.

in the project, but she refused. She never wanted to have anything to do with building bombs. She was greatly saddened that scientists would use her discoveries for such destructive purposes.

In 1944, Otto Hahn was awarded the Nobel Prize in chemistry for discovering nuclear fission. Unfortunately, the Nobel committee ignored Lise's contribution to the discovery. This was partly because Lise hadn't actually been in Berlin with Otto when he did his experiments, and partly because Otto downplayed her role in the discovery. Today, many people believe that the Nobel Prize should have gone to Lise, too.

Still, Lise Meitner became world famous for her work in helping unlock the secrets of the atom. Over the years, nuclear fission was also used for peaceful purposes, like generating electric power for the world's energy needs.

Lise Meitner continued her nuclear experiments for many years. She received many honors and awards for her work, and lived a long life. Lise died peacefully in Cambridge, England, in 1968, at the age of 89. In 1997, a new element was named *Meitnerium* in honor of Lise.

In 1959, Lise Meitner came to the United States to lecture at Bryn Mawr College, in Pennsylvania. Here she is shown with some Bryn Mawr students.

# Glossary

**atom** (AT-uhm) The tiniest part of an element that has all the properties of that element; everything is made up of atoms

**atomic bomb** (uh-TOM-ik BOM) A powerful bomb, the explosion of which results from the energy released when atoms split apart

**dictator** (DIK-tay-tur) Someone who has complete control of a country, often ruling it unjustly

**electron** (i-LEK-tron) A tiny particle that moves around the nucleus of an atom; electrons carry a negative electrical charge

**element** (EL-uh-muhnt) In chemistry, a pure substance that cannot be chemically broken down into a simpler substance

**matter** (MAT-ur) Anything that has weight and takes up space

**neutron** (NOO-tron) One of the extremely small parts in the nucleus of an atom; neutrons have no electrical charge

**nuclear fission** (NOO-klee-uhr FISH-uhn) The splitting of the nucleus of an atom, resulting in the release of large amounts of energy

**nuclear physics** ( FIZ-iks) Physics is the science that deals with matter and energy; nuclear physics is the branch of physics that studies the central parts of atoms

**nucleus** (NOO-klee-uhss) The central part of an atom

**particles** (PAR-tuh-kuhlz) In physics, the minute parts of atoms

**prejudice** (PREJ-uh-diss) Hatred or unfair treatment that results from having fixed opinions about some group of people

**proton** (PROH-ton) One of the extremely small parts in the nucleus of an atom; protons carry a positive electrical charge

**radioactivity** (ray-dee-oh-ack-TIV-ih-tee) The release of energy that occurs when the central parts of certain atoms break apart

# Index